Nuts about
CHOCOLATE

Recipes by
Susan Mendelson &
Deborah Roitberg

For Maureen —
Open up; dig in!!
Deborah Roitberg

Happy Cooking
Susan Mendelson

Douglas & McIntyre
Vancouver/Toronto

Dedicated to our mothers, Jeanette and Roz, who taught us that a bargain is not a bargain unless you need it.

Douglas & McIntyre Ltd.
1615 Venables Street
Vancouver, British Columbia
V5L 2H1

Canadian Cataloguing in Publication Data

Mendelson, Susan, 1952–
Nuts about chocolate

Includes index.
ISBN 0-88894-407-1

1. Cookery (Chocolate) 2. Cookery (Nuts)
I. Roitberg, Deborah, 1951–   II. Title.
TX767.C5M45   641.6'374   C83-091283-5

Design by Barbara Hodgson
Photography by Derik Murray
Typeset by Evergreen Press
Printed and bound in Canada by Agency Press

CONTENTS

Never trust anyone who tells you they don't eat desserts. You know, those people who look at you smugly when you offer your *pièce de résistance* and say, "Oh, I couldn't; this dessert is too rich!" We simply respond with, "We don't understand the concept of 'too rich' — or 'too chocolaty' for that matter." Our approach is "Eat and enjoy!" *But* only indulge if it's worth every calorie.

Think about all the *chazarai* (junk food) you consume daily that you don't even think about, let alone enjoy. Then imagine a perfect wedge of cointreau fudge cake before you . . . or a mint truffle torte, a frosty butter pecan mousse. Even a whole chocolate amaretto cheesecake. Are you really going to stop and worry about calories? Get serious!

In the last year we tested and tasted over five hundred dessert recipes, many several times. We might as well have taken the chocolate and applied it directly to our thighs. What, you may ask, did we do it for? To save you the unnecessary inches. The recipes that were not worth the calories we discarded; the ones that remain are those which you can serve with no sense of guilt, no self-recrimination — only a tremendous sense of pride when you tell your friends you made them yourself and a feeling of pleasure knowing you can indulge to the limit without a trace of anxiety. Have another slice . . . Enjoy!

Susan & Deborah

Acknowledgements

For those who shared their secrets, and sacrificed their diets to help us test these recipes, we want to thank: Lynn Mendelson, Mother Jeanette, Mother Roz, Grandma Faye Bigman, Peter Thompson, Grandpa Joe Bigman, Roberta Braidner, Barbara Cohen, Shelley Comer, Alison Delosky, Anna de Flores, Joe Grice, Miriam Gropper, Martha Katz, Barbara Larabie, Lois Lilienstein, Moira North, Marián Paris, Carol Roitberg, Shelley Scott, Kurtis Strelau, and Diddy Thompson. A special thanks to our wonderful staff and devoted customers, and to Martha Miller for giving our book the perfect title.

WORKING WITH CHOCOLATE

There are three things to keep in mind when working with chocolate:
1 Chocolate burns easily.
2 Water, even a drop, added to chocolate can cause problems.
3 Chocolate may not be chocolate.

Here are our recommendations:

When melting chocolate, chop it into uniform bits; place in the top of a *clean, completely dry* double boiler over HOT not BOILING water. NEVER COVER. When the chocolate is almost melted, remove from the heat and stir until just melted.

If a drop or two of moisture should land on the chocolate, it can cause the chocolate to "tighten" or "seize." Don't panic. Stir in about a teaspoon of vegetable oil or shortening per ounce (*30 g*) of chocolate, and all will be saved.

Always read labels when buying chocolate to make sure you are getting the real thing. Pure chocolate has been made with either chocolate liqueur or cocoa butter. Anything else is a "chocolate flavoured" synthetic.

PLAYING WITH CHOCOLATE

Chocolate Curls

To make these decorations, melt semi-sweet chocolate together with a tsp. of oil for each 2 oz. (*60 g*) of chocolate and pour onto a flat surface. (We prefer a cold marble slab, but any flat surface will do.) Spread the chocolate so that it is even and very thin. When it starts to lose its shine and is firm but not hard, it's time to start the curls. Holding a metal spatula (a pancake flipper works well) at a 45° angle, push against the chocolate until it forms a large curl. (The motion is a little like shovelling snow.) Let the curls dry until firm, then store in an airtight container in a cool place. Use the spatula to lift the curls into the container; fingerprints will leave marks on the chocolate.

Smaller curls can be made using a vegetable peeler against a block of chocolate (at room temperature); this works especially well with the softer chocolates such as European fondants. To avoid marking the chocolate, hold the block with waxed paper.

Chocolate Flowers

Cut three sheets of waxed paper, 6″ × 1½″ (*15 cm × 2.5 cm*). Melt the chocolate and paint it onto the paper using a pastry brush. Refrigerate until firm but not hard — about 5 minutes. Carefully peel the chocolate off the paper, curling it around itself as tightly as possible. Continue until you have a flower of the desired size. If it is not exactly to your liking, throw the chocolate back into the pot and start again.

Chocolate Leaves

Flat, waxy leaves like those from camellia bushes make the best moulds. Clean and dry them well. Melt semi-sweet chocolate and, using a pastry brush, paint the chocolate on the *underside* of the leaf, coating evenly. Wipe away any excess chocolate from the front or sides of the leaf. Place on a sheet of waxed paper, uncoated side down, in the refrigerator for 8–10 minutes, until chocolate is hardened. Beginning at the stem end, carefully peel away the leaf. Voila! A magnificent chocolate leaf. For a professional look, handle as little as possible.

CAUTION: Be sure the leaf you use is nontoxic.

INGREDIENTS & PREPARATION

In our recipes we use all-purpose flour, light vegetable oil (our preference is for cold-pressed sunflower oil), white granulated sugar (unless otherwise specified), fresh lemon juice (although bottled juice can be substituted if absolutely necessary), and pure vanilla extract. Liquid and solid honey are interchangeable — we usually use liquid — and when brown sugar is called for it can be either light or dark. Butter can be salted or unsalted, but we prefer unsalted since it lets the other flavours come through. When a recipe requires the butter to be creamed, it should be brought to room temperature first. Eggs should always be room temperature before using.

Bitter chocolate is unsweetened; bittersweet chocolate is semi-sweet. To cut chocolate that has hardened, first score the surface with a very sharp knife, then cut through it. This method will prevent cracking.

Always toast nuts before chopping them, but watch that they do not burn. Spread the nuts on a cookie sheet, place in a 350°F (*180°C*) oven and toast as follows:

Walnuts	7–8 minutes
Pecans	7–8 minutes
Peanuts	12–15 minutes
Hazelnuts	14–15 minutes
Almonds	16–18 minutes

Flaked nuts take less toasting time than whole ones.

To prepare pans, either smear with butter and dust flour over the surface until the butter is well-coated *or* line the pan with waxed paper cut to the size of its bottom.

CHOCOLATE

Cointreau Fudge Cake

Preheat oven to 350°F (*180°C*)

1½ cups (*375 mL*) soft butter 6 oz. (*170 g*) soft cream cheese 3 cups (*750 mL*) light brown sugar	Using electric mixer, cream butter and cream cheese. Gradually add sugar until mixture is light and fluffy.
5 eggs	Add eggs one at a time, mixing after each addition.
4 oz. (*115 g*) unsweetened chocolate, melted and slightly cooled	Add.
1 cup (*250 mL*) buttermilk or yogurt	Add all at once. (The mixture will look as if it's curdling, but not to worry.)
3 cups (*750 mL*) flour 2½ Tbsp. (*40 mL*) orange rind, finely grated	Gradually add and blend well.

1 cup (*250 mL*) boiling water 2 tsp. (*10 mL*) baking soda 2 Tbsp. (*30 mL*) Cointreau liqueur	Combine and fold into batter.

Pour into three prepared, round 9″ (*22 cm*) cake pans. Bake for 25–30 minutes until toothpick comes out clean. Let sit for 30 minutes in pans before removing. Ice and chill.

Cointreau Icing

½ cup (*125 mL*) soft butter	Cream until smooth.
1 cup (*250 mL*) soft cream cheese	Add and beat well.
4 oz. (*115 g*) unsweetened chocolate, melted and slightly cooled	Add.
4 cups (*1 L*) icing sugar	Add.
2 Tbsp. (*30 mL*) Cointreau 2 Tbsp. (*30 mL*) orange juice concentrate Rind of one orange, finely grated	Add and beat until fluffy.

This amount will fill and frost top and sides of a three-layer cake.

Chocolate and orange are wonderfully complementary flavours and when added to both cake and icing, the result is irresistible.

Double Fudge Chocolate Cake

Preheat oven to 350°F (*180°C*)

2 eggs 1 cup (*250 mL*) sugar 2 Tbsp. (*30 mL*) soft butter 1 cup (*250 mL*) oil ½ cup (*125 mL*) cocoa, packed ½ cup (*125 mL*) buttermilk 1 tsp. (*5 mL*) vanilla	Beat in this order, adding ingredients one at a time.
2¼ cups (*550 mL*) flour 1½ tsp. (*7 mL*) baking soda 1½ tsp (*7 mL*) baking powder	Sift together and add to above mixture.
1 cup (*250 mL*) boiling water	Fold in.

½ cup (*125 mL*) chocolate chips

Place mixture in two prepared, round 8″ or 9″ (*20–22 cm*) cake pans. Sprinkle with chocolate chips. Bake for 25 minutes. Ice with our Incredible Chocolate Icing.

For years, this was our guarded secret. Our customers call it The Definitive Chocolate Cake. As a double bonus, you now get our Incredible Chocolate Icing recipe.

Incredible Chocolate Icing

½ cup (*125 mL*) soft butter
1 cup (*250 mL*) icing sugar
⅔ cup (*150 mL*) cocoa

Place in food processor and, using steel knife, blend for 4 seconds.

1 tsp. (*5 mL*) vanilla
2 Tbsp. (*30 mL*) milk
2 Tbsp. (*30 mL*) hot coffee

Add liquid and blend until smooth. Additional milk will make a thinner icing.

You can combine these ingredients with an electric mixer, but the texture will not be as smooth.

White Chocolate Icing

1½ cups (*375 mL*) soft butter
½ cup (*125 mL*) icing sugar

Beat until smooth.
Gradually beat into butter.

8 oz. (*250 g*) white chocolate, melted and slightly cooled
½ tsp (*2 mL*) vanilla

Slowly add to above.

Yield: 4 cups (*1 L*).

Rich, rich, rich! Fabulous on Double Fudge Chocolate Cake!

Chocolate Mousse Cake

Chocolate Sponge

Preheat oven to 350°F *(180°C)*.

6 eggs
¾ cup *(175 mL)* sugar

Combine. Heat in top of double boiler until lukewarm over hot, NOT BOILING, water. Now beat with electric mixer until triple in volume.

½ cup *(125 mL)* flour
⅓ cup *(75 mL)* cocoa

Sift flour and cocoa and fold one-third at a time into eggs.

⅓ cup *(75 mL)* butter, melted and slightly cooled

Carefully fold butter one-fourth at a time into mixture.

Pour onto prepared cookie sheet or jellyroll pan and bake for 20 minutes.

1 Chocolate Mousse recipe (page 13)
1 Lazy Gourmet Glaze recipe (page 13)

To Assemble

Line loaf pan with plastic wrap leaving about a 2″ *(5 cm)* overhang on all sides. Cut chocolate sponge into six pieces, one to cover the pan bottom, one for each side and one to enclose the top. Place cake along bottom and sides of loaf pan. Fill with mousse and place final sponge layer on top, pressing down slightly. Wrap with plastic and chill 3–4 hours or overnight. Unwrap and set on wire rack. Gently pour glaze over top and sides of loaf. Decorate with whipped cream, or orange peel if Cointreau has been used, or cherries if mousse has been made with kirsch.

The state of the art in desserts.

Unbelievable Chocolate Mousse

2 cups (*500 mL*) chocolate chips	Process in food processor for 5 seconds.
⅓ cup (*75 mL*) boiling water	Add slowly and continue to process.
5 egg yolks 3 Tbsp. (*45 mL*) brandy 4 Tbsp. (*60 mL*) soft sweet butter	Add yolks one at a time. Add brandy. Add butter, a little at a time.
5 egg whites	Beat egg whites until stiff, then gently fold into chocolate. (We like to first add a little of the whites to the chocolate to lighten the texture and then add the rest of the whites.)
	Chill 3–4 hours before serving, or use in other recipes.

Variations

For Chocolate Orange Mousse use 3 Tbsp. (*45 mL*) orange-flavoured liqueur.

For Hazelnut Mousse use 3 Tbsp. (*45 mL*) frangelico and top with crushed hazelnuts.

For Mocha Mousse use 3 Tbsp. (*45 mL*) coffee-flavoured liqueur.

Once you have this recipe down pat, it will take only 10 minutes to make.

The Lazy Gourmet Glaze

¼ cup (*50 mL*) butter 4 oz. (*115 g*) semi-sweet chocolate	Melt together.
2 Tbsp. (*30 mL*) heavy cream 1 Tbsp. (*15 mL*) coffee liqueur	Mix well and add to chocolate.

Your Basic Chocolate Cheesecake

Preheat oven to 350°F (*180°C*).

Chocolate Crust

1⅓ cups (*325 mL*) chocolate wafers, crushed ⅓ cup (*75 mL*) melted butter	Mix and press into a 9″ or 10″ (*22–25 cm*) springform pan. Bake for 5 minutes.
1 lb. (*500 g*) soft cream cheese ⅔ cup (*150 mL*) sour cream ½ cup (*125 mL*) sugar 2 tsp. (*10 mL*) vanilla	Combine and beat until smooth.
6 oz. (*170 g*) semi-sweet chocolate 1 oz. (*30 g*) bitter chocolate	Melt over hot water and add to mixture, beating until smooth.
2 large eggs	Add and beat for 5 minutes.

Pour mixture into crust. Bake 35–40 minutes. Let sit until cake reaches room temperature, then chill 2 hours.

Variations

Omit vanilla and add in its place:

1 Tbsp. (*15 mL*) brandy	For Chocolate Brandy Cheesecake
1 Tbsp. (*15 mL*) orange juice concentrate 1 Tbsp. (*15 mL*) orange liqueur	For Chocolate Orange Cheesecake
1 Tbsp. (*15 mL*) almond liqueur 1 tsp. (*5 mL*) almond extract	For Chocolate Amaretto Cheesecake

Toppings

For Your Basic Chocolate Cheesecake:

1 cup (*250 mL*) heavy cream 2 Tbsp. (*30 mL*) icing sugar 1 tsp. (*5 mL*) vanilla	Beat until soft peaks form. Spread over chilled chocolate. Chill 1 hour before serving.

For Sour Cream Topping:

1 cup (*250 mL*) sour cream
1 Tbsp. (*15 mL*) your favourite flavouring
2 Tbsp. (*30 mL*) sugar
} Mix and spoon gently over cheesecake and return to oven for 5 minutes.

Sprinkle with shaved chocolate and/or nuts. Chill 2–3 hours before serving.

The combination of cheese and chocolate may at first sound peculiar, but this cheesecake will change your concept about life in general!

Bittersweet Cubes

Cake

Prepare Chocolate Sponge
(page 12)

Filling: Ganache

2 cups (*500 mL*) heavy cream	Heat until boiling; remove from heat.
10 oz. (*280 g*) semi-sweet chocolate chips *or* chocolate, finely grated	Vigorously blend chocolate with hot cream.
2 Tbsp. (*30 mL*) coffee liqueur	Add liqueur.
	Chill well. When cold, beat until thick.

Mirror Glaze (page 31)

Cut cake in half and spread with Ganache. Top with other half. With serrated knife, cut into 24 cubes — but do not separate. Spread with glaze. Chill 1 hour, then cut all the way through.

Gorgeous with afternoon tea.

Chocolate Mousse Roll

Preheat oven to 350°F (*180°C*).

4 Tbsp. (*60 mL*) flour 4 Tbsp. (*60 mL*) cocoa 1 tsp. (*5 mL*) baking powder	Sift together and set aside.
5 egg whites	Beat until stiff.
½ cup (*125 mL*) sugar	Gradually add sugar to egg whites and set aside.
5 egg yolks ½ cup (*125 mL*) sugar	Beat yolks until thick. Add sugar gradually.
1½ Tbsp. (*25 mL*) cold water 1 tsp. (*5 mL*) vanilla	Add water and vanilla to yolks.
	Now fold one-third whites into yolks, then sift one-third flour mixture over the eggs.
	Gently fold rest of whites into mixture and add remainder of flour in small amounts while folding.

Pour into jelly roll pan that has been lined with waxed paper and bake for 20 minutes until sponge springs back when touched lightly. Cool and turn out onto a clean tea towel which has been lightly sprinkled with icing sugar. Roll lengthwise and chill. Unroll and fill with 2 cups (*500 mL*) (½ recipe) Chocolate Mousse (page 13).

or

Fill with 2 cups (*500 mL*) whipped cream — 1 cup (*250 mL*) heavy cream — combined with 1 Tbsp. (*15 mL*) icing sugar and 1 Tbsp. (*15 mL*) liqueur.

or Fill with ice cream.

Ice with Lazy Gourmet Glaze (page 13).

Serve with Raspberry Sauce (page 59) or Hot Fudge Sauce (page 37) — or both!

Cointreau Fudge Cake and Cointreau Icing (pages 8, 9)

White Chocolate Mousse

12 oz. (*340 g*) white chocolate	Melt, then allow to cool until warm.
3 cups (*750 mL*) heavy cream	Whip cream and set aside. (Cream should be stiff.)
4 egg yolks ¾ cup (*175 mL*) sugar	In large bowl beat yolks until pale yellow, then add sugar gradually.
2 pkgs. gelatine (2 Tbsp./*30 mL*) ¼ cup (*50 mL*) warm water	Soften gelatine in water. Heat to dissolve if necessary.
	Add a small amount of egg yolk mixture to gelatine, then combine gelatine mixture with yolks and beat vigorously.
	Gradually add melted chocolate, using low speed on food processor or electric mixer. (If mixture is not completely smooth, reheat in double boiler to dissolve lumps.) Then gently add whipped cream.

Chill until set. Serve topped with toasted almonds or fresh berries in season.

This exotic version can be layered with our dark chocolate mousse for an interesting display of textures, but — each layer must be thoroughly chilled before adding the next.

Black Forest Cherry Torte (page 20)

Black Forest Cherry Torte

Genoise

	Preheat oven to 350°F (*180°C*).
6 eggs	Beat 8–10 minutes until very light and fluffy.
1 cup (*250 mL*) sugar 1 tsp. (*5 mL*) vanilla	Add to eggs very gradually, beating on high.
½ cup (*125 mL*) flour ½ cup (*125 mL*) cocoa	Sift a little at a time over eggs and fold in.
10 Tbsp. (*150 mL*) butter, melted and slightly cooled	Add, 2 Tbsp. (*30 mL*) at a time, folding in gently.

Prepare three round 8″ or 9″ (*20–22 cm*) cake pans. Gently pour mixture into the pans, dividing equally. Bake for 10–15 minutes.

Syrup

¾ cup (*175 mL*) sugar 1 cup (*250 mL*) cold water	Combine in saucepan. Bring to a boil and continue to boil for 5 minutes. Remove from stove.
⅓ cup (*75 mL*) kirsch	When room temperature, add kirsch. Prick layers and gently pour syrup over each.

Cream Filling

3 cups (*750 mL*) chilled heavy cream ½ cup (*125 mL*) icing sugar ¼ cup (*50 mL*) kirsch	Beat cream until thick; add sugar and kirsch gradually.
1 cup (*250 mL*) pitted bing cherries (Use fresh fruit in season)	

To Assemble

Start with a layer of cake. Place ½ cup (*125 mL*) cherries on cake;

spread with one-third cream filling. Add another layer of cake, remaining cherries and one-third cream filling. Top with third layer and spread remaining cream on top and sides. Decorate with chocolate curls (page 5).

The ultimate Black Forest cake.

German Chocolate Cake

Chocolate Genoise (page 20) Make Genoise in three round 8″ or 9″ (*20–22 cm*) cake pans.

Filling

1 egg
½ cup (*125 mL*) sugar
1 Tbsp. (*15 mL*) flour
1 cup (*250 mL*) sour cream
½ cup (*125 mL*) raisins, coarsely chopped with
1 Tbsp. (*15 mL*) flour

Mix in top of double boiler and cook over medium heat until thick, stirring constantly. Let cool 15 minutes.

½ cup (*125 mL*) threaded coconut, toasted
½ cup (*125 mL*) pecans, coarsely chopped
1 tsp. (*5 mL*) vanilla
1 tsp. (*5 mL*) lemon juice

Add to above.

Makes about 2½ cups (*625 mL*).

Incredible Chocolate Icing
(page 11)

To Assemble

Spread layers and top of Genoise with filling. Ice sides and if you're feeling wicked, decorate with rosettes of icing.

Mint Truffle Torte

Chocolate Genoise (page 20)

Make Genoise in three round 8″ or 9″ (20–22 cm) cake pans. With fork or toothpicks make holes in Genoise and pour mint syrup over.

Mint Syrup

1 cup (250 mL) sugar
1 cup (250 mL) water
1½ oz. (45 g) bitter chocolate, grated

Bring to boil.
Add to sugar mixture and stir until chocolate is melted.

1½ tsp. (7 mL) peppermint extract

Add.

When syrup reaches room temperature, pour over Genoise.

Crème Ganache

2 cups (500 mL) heavy cream

Bring to boil; remove from heat.

12 oz. (340 g) semi-sweet chocolate, grated or 12 oz. (340 g) chocolate chips

Pour chocolate into cream and whisk vigorously until well blended.

½ cup (125 mL) Crème de Menthe

Add liqueur.

Chill. When cold, whip until smooth and thick.

To Assemble

Start with a layer of syrup-filled cake. Spread with ganache. Add another layer of cake, then another layer of ganache. End with a layer of cake. Ice top and sides with ganache and decorate with rosettes of ganache or green mints.

This torte is better after sitting for a day or two, but you'll have to hide it or risk being the victim of the great chocolate disappearing act.

Chocolate Decadence Torte

Preheat oven to 425°F (*220°C*).

1 lb. (*500 g*) semi-sweet chocolate ¾ cup (*175 mL*) butter	Melt together in double boiler, then pour into bowl and set aside.
4 eggs 2 tsp. (*10 mL*) sugar	In clean double boiler, combine and place over hot water; heat until warm. Then beat on high speed until cool and quadrupled in volume (about 8–10 minutes).
1 Tbsp. (*15 mL*) flour	Sift over egg mixture and fold in.
2 tsp. (*10 mL*) vanilla	Fold in.
	Gently fold one-third egg mixture into chocolate mixture, then fold in remaining eggs.

Carefully pour into prepared 8″ or 9″ (*20–22 cm*) springform pan. Bake for 15 minutes. (It will sink a bit in the centre. DON'T WORRY!) Let cool and then freeze immediately.

To Decorate

1 cup (*250 mL*) heavy cream 1 Tbsp. (*15 mL*) icing sugar	Whip to soft peaks.

Place sweetened cream in pastry bag with star tip and play! Serve chilled.

This recipe has swept North America as the indulgent dessert. We sometimes serve it with raspberry sauce (page 59) to cut the richness.

Chocolate Pastry

1 cup (*250 mL*) flour ¼ cup (*50 mL*) brown sugar 3 Tbsp. (*45 mL*) cocoa }	Combine.
½ cup (*125 mL*) cold butter	Cut into pieces, then cut with food processor or two knives or pastry blender into flour mixture until coarse pieces form.
2 Tbsp. (*30 mL*) milk 1 tsp. (*5 mL*) vanilla }	Add to mixture and combine until just blended.

Pat into 9″ or 10″ (*23–25 cm*) pie plate, crimping edges for nice design.

A delicious crust that needs no patchka *(rolling out).*

No-Fail Pastry

2½ cups (*600 mL*) flour ½ lb. (*250 g*) shortening }	Cut shortening into flour until coarse pieces form.
or ¼ lb. (*125 g*) butter and ¼ lb. (*125 g*) shortening	
1 egg water juice of 1 lemon }	Combine to make ½ cup (*125 mL*). Add to flour mixture.

Roll out to desired thickness. Makes enough pastry for a two-crust pie.

Chocolate Heaven Pie

9″ or 10″ (*23–25 cm*) Chocolate Crust (page 24)	Prebake at 400°F (*200°C*) for 10 minutes.
2 egg whites 1½ tsp. (*7 mL*) vinegar ½ tsp. (*2 mL*) salt 1 tsp. (*5 mL*) cinnamon	Combine and beat until soft peaks form.
½ cup (*125 mL*) sugar	Gradually add sugar until stiff peaks form.
	Spread over pie shell and bake at 325°F (*160°C*) for 15–18 minutes until brown. Cool.
⅓ cup (*75 mL*) Bittersweet Fudge Sauce (page 37)	Drizzle with sauce.
1 cup (*250 mL*) heavy cream	Beat cream.
⅓ cup (*75 mL*) chocolate chips, melted and slightly cooled 1 egg yolk 1 Tbsp. (*15 mL*) milk	Add chocolate, yolk and milk and beat until thick. Spread over sauce.
1 cup (*250 mL*) heavy cream ½ tsp. (*2 mL*) cinnamon ¼ cup (*50 mL*) icing sugar	Beat until soft peaks form. Spread over chocolate, or pipe using pastry bag with large tip for a professional look.
½ cup (*125 mL*) chocolate chips	Decorate with chocolate curls (page 5).
	Chill.

Heaven on earth!

Magnificent Mint Mousse Pie

Preheat oven to 350°F (*180°C*).

Chocolate Mousse Base

2 Tbsp. (*30 mL*) cookie crumbs, preferably chocolate	Sprinkle over 9″ (*23 cm*) buttered glass pie plate.
8 oz. (*250 g*) semi-sweet chocolate ¼ cup (*50 mL*) hot water	In top of double boiler melt together. Stir gently until smooth. Cool slightly.
5 egg yolks	In separate bowl, beat yolks until thick and pale.
¼ cup (*50 mL*) sugar	Add sugar and beat 5 minutes.
½ tsp. (*2 mL*) vanilla	Add vanilla.
	Fold three-quarters of chocolate mixture into yolks and pour into pie plate, covering sides as well as possible. Set remaining mixture aside.

Bake for 18–20 minutes. (The filling will sink a bit while cooling.)

Mint Filling

1 envelope gelatine ½ cup (*125 mL*) milk	Soften gelatine in cold milk, then dissolve over low heat.
3 egg yolks ¼ cup (*50 mL*) sugar	Beat together, then add gelatine mixture and beat until slightly thickened. Chill until mixture is the consistency of mayonnaise — approximately ½ hour.
¼ cup (*50 mL*) green crème de menthe ¼ cup (*50 mL*) white crème de cacao 2 drops of green food colouring	Add to above and set aside.

1 cup (*250 mL*) heavy cream	Beat until stiff and set aside.
3 egg whites ¼ cup (*50 mL*) sugar	Beat until soft peaks form. Gradually add sugar, beating until stiff peaks form.
	Now gently fold cream into green mixture, then fold in egg whites.
2 Tbsp. (*30 mL*) hot water	Add the water to the reserved chocolate crust mixture, then add ½ cup (*125 mL*) of the green mixture.
	Pour green mixture over the cooled crust. Swirl the remaining chocolate mixture over the top.
	Chill 3–4 hours until firm.

This pie is actually very easy to make. It just takes a lot of words to explain!

Chocolate Cherry Dome Pie

8 oz. (*250 g*) pitted cherries
(Use fresh when in season)
3 Tbsp. (*45 mL*) kirsch } Soak ahead at least 1 hour.

Prepare 10″ (*25 cm*) pie shell (either chocolate or plain pastry) and bake at 350°F (*180°C*) for 20 minutes.

1 cup (*250 mL*) soft butter
¾ cup (*175 mL*) icing sugar } Combine in bowl and beat with electric mixer on high speed until fluffy.

½ cup (*125 mL*) cocoa — Sift in cocoa and blend.

8 oz. (*250 g*) semi-sweet chocolate, melted and slightly cooled — Add slowly to cocoa mixture, beating in.

1 egg — Beat in.

1 cup (*250 mL*) heavy cream — Add and beat until very fluffy — at least 5 minutes.

Add kirsch in which cherries were soaked.

Pour three-quarters of mixture into pastry shell. Press cherries into surface. Cover with rest of chocolate mixture, creating a dome effect.

4 oz. (*115 g*) semi-sweet chocolate
½ tsp. (*2 mL*) butter } Melt in double boiler. Let cool and gently pour over pie.

With a sharp knife score sections to be cut (about 14). Chill.

Even lighter than our mousse!

Neapolitan Torte

Preheat oven to 350°F (*180°C*).

1 egg 1 cup (*250 mL*) sugar }	Beat together.
1 cup (*250 mL*) butter, melted and slightly cooled	Add.
2½ cups (*625 mL*) flour ⅛ tsp. (*0.5 mL*) baking soda }	Sift together.
	Mix all together. Knead slightly.

Divide into four prepared round 8″ or 9″ (*20–22 cm*) pans and bake for 15–18 minutes, until golden brown. Cool slightly before removing from pans.

Chocolate Filling

3 egg yolks ¾ cup (*175 mL*) sugar }	Mix together in saucepan.
¼ cup (*50 mL*) cocoa 2¼ cups (*550 mL*) milk }	Add cocoa and milk and bring to a boil.
¼ cup (*50 mL*) cornstarch dissolved in ¾ cup (*175 mL*) milk }	Add and whisk until smooth and thick.
1½ Tbsp. (*25 mL*) butter 1 tsp. (*5 mL*) vanilla }	Add and let cool. Stir frequently.

When cake and custard are cool, spread filling between layers and over top. *Chill for at least 24 hours.*

A Bar Mitzvah sweet-table standard delight. Always the first to go.

Cassata

Filling

3 cups (*750 mL*) ricotta cheese ¾ cup (*175 mL*) sugar	Blend together.
1½ Tbsp. (*25 mL*) grated orange peel 4 oz. (*115 g*) semi-sweet chocolate, finely chopped	Add and blend.
	Set aside and chill.
	Preheat oven to 350°F (*180°C*).

Italian Sponge Cake

4 egg whites	Beat until soft peaks form.
¼ cup (*50 mL*) sugar	Gradually add sugar and beat until stiff peaks form.
4 egg yolks	In separate bowl beat yolks until light.
⅓ cup (*75 mL*) sugar	Gradually add sugar to yolks and beat. Gently fold whites into yolks.
¾ cup (*175 mL*) flour 1 tsp. (*5 mL*) baking powder	Sift over egg mixture and gently fold in.

Pour into prepared loaf pan and bake for 35 minutes. Invert on rack to cool.

Syrup

⅓ cup (*75 mL*) sugar ⅓ cup (*75 mL*) water	Combine in saucepan over medium heat and let boil for 30 seconds. Remove from heat and cool for 5 minutes.

2 Tbsp. (*30 mL*) Cointreau or
orange liqueur } Add to cooled mixture.
2 Tbsp. (*30 mL*) brandy

Incredible Chocolate Icing
(page 11)

To Assemble

Slice cake horizontally into three layers. Brush each layer with syrup. Spread first layer with half the ricotta. Spread the second layer with remaining ricotta. Ice with Incredible Chocolate Icing. Decorate with pine nuts or pistachios.

An authentic Sicilian dessert. As they say in Italy, "O pancia mia! Fatti capanna!" (Oh, belly of mine! Make yourself a warehouse!)

Mirror Glaze

½ cup (*125 mL*) strong coffee } Combine in heavy saucepan and
⅓ cup (*75 mL*) sugar } heat until sugar is melted.

6 oz. (*170 g*) semi-sweet
chocolate — Chop coarsely and add.

2 Tbsp. (*30 mL*) light corn
syrup — Add and boil for 5 minutes, then remove from heat.

2 Tbsp. (*30 mL*) butter
2 Tbsp. (*30 mL*) coffee- } Add butter and liqueur and beat
flavoured liqueur } until mixture thickens.

Spread on cake immediately. Makes just under 1½ cups (*375 mL*).

This stores well. Just reheat in double boiler and beat again.

Zuccotto Florentino

Make sponge cake as in Cassata (page 30) but bake in round 9" (*22 cm*) pan.

Make Cointreau Syrup as in Cassata (page 30).

Filling #1

1 tsp. (*5 mL*) gelatine 1 Tbsp. (*15 mL*) cold water	Dissolve in double boiler over hot water and stir to melt.
1½ cups (*375 mL*) heavy cream ¼ cup (*50 mL*) icing sugar	Beat until soft peaks form. Then add gelatine mixture and continue beating until firm peaks form.
3 oz. (*85 g*) semi-sweet chocolate, coarsely chopped 2 Tbsp. (*30 mL*) Cointreau or orange liqueur	Add.

Filling #2

1½ cups (*375 mL*) heavy cream	Beat until stiff peaks form.
6 oz. (*170 g*) semi-sweet chocolate, melted and cooled slightly	Add chocolate to cream in slow stream.
2 Tbsp. (*30 mL*) brandy	Add.
½ cup (*125 mL*) chopped almonds, toasted	Fold in.
Mirror Glaze (page 31)	

To Assemble

Line 2½ qt. (*2½ L*) bowl with plastic wrap. Divide cake horizontally into three layers. Set top of cake, cut side up, into bowl. Brush with syrup, using pastry brush. Spread Cointreau cream (Filling #1) over cake. Place middle layer of cake over cream. Brush with syrup.

Spread with chocolate cream (Filling #2). Brush cut side of final layer with remaining syrup and press against chocolate cream. Chill for three hours or overnight. Top with glaze. Chill. Remove from refrigerator 15 minutes before serving.

An awe-inspiring presentation. Don't tell your guests how simple it is to make.

Just Like Chocolate Ice Cream

	Oil a 2 qt. (*2 L*) soufflé dish. Make a 2″ (*5 cm*) foil collar and wrap it around the top of the dish. Seal with tape.
8 egg yolks	Beat with electric beater until lemon-coloured.
¾ cup (*175 mL*) sugar	Gradually add sugar and beat until light and fluffy. Set aside.
2 envelopes gelatine ⅓ cup (*75 mL*) cold strong coffee 8 oz. (*250 g*) semi-sweet chocolate, melted and slightly cooled ½ cup (*125 mL*) coffee liqueur	Soften gelatine in coffee, then dissolve over low heat and add to chocolate. Add liqueur. Now add mixture to yolks.
8 egg whites	Beat until stiff and gently fold into chocolate mixture.
2 cups (*500 mL*) heavy cream 1 Tbsp. (*15 mL*) icing sugar	Beat until soft peaks form and fold in.
2 oz. (*60 g*) semi-sweet chocolate, coarsely chopped	Fold into mixture and pour into soufflé dish.

Freeze for 3–4 hours. Let stand in refrigerator 1 hour before serving.

Chocolate Rapture

Preheat oven to 325°F (*160°C*).

½ cup (*125 mL*) butter 4 oz. (*115 g*) semi-sweet chocolate 2 oz. (*60 g*) bitter chocolate	Melt in double boiler. Remove from heat.
½ cup (*125 mL*) sugar 3 Tbsp. (*45 mL*) flour 4 egg yolks	Add to above in this order.
4 egg whites	Beat until stiff peaks form, then gently fold into chocolate mixture.

Pour into prepared 9″ (*22 cm*) springform pan and bake for 25 minutes. Cool, then chill.

1 cup (*250 mL*) heavy cream	Beat until soft peaks form.
1 Tbsp. (*15 mL*) icing sugar 1 Tbsp. (*15 mL*) coffee-flavoured liqueur	Add to cream and spread over cake.
	Chill for 2 hours.
Hot Fudge Sauce (page 37) *or* Mirror Glaze (page 31)	Spoon sauce or glaze over cake and place in freezer ½ hour or longer. Remove from freezer 10 minutes before serving.

A dessert can never be too rich or too light. This one manages both.

Cassata with pine nut garnish (page 30)

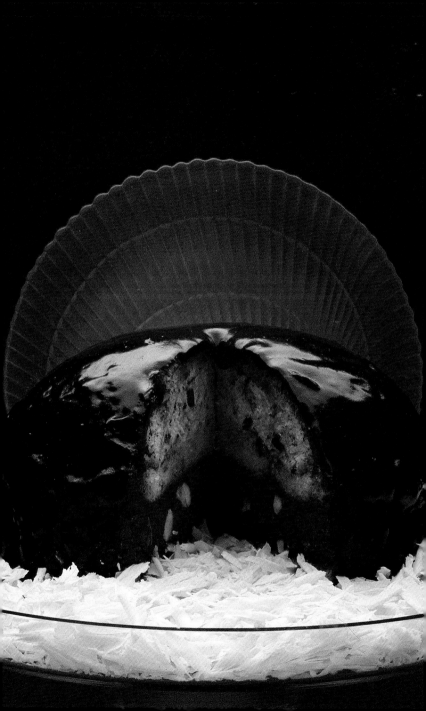

Bittersweet Hot Fudge Sauce

1 cup (*250 mL*) sugar ¾ cup (*175 mL*) cocoa 1½ Tbsp. (*25 mL*) instant coffee	Combine in saucepan.
½ cup (*125 mL*) heavy cream	Add and blend to a smooth paste.
½ cup (*125 mL*) heavy cream	Add and blend well.
	Place mixture over medium heat and stir until sugar is dissolved.
2 Tbsp. (*30 mL*) butter	Add butter. Cook, stirring, for 6–7 minutes. Remove from heat at once.

Keep chilled and reheat to serve. This sauce also freezes well.

Chocolate Fudge

⅔ cup (*150 mL*) cocoa 3 cups (*750 mL*) sugar 1½ cups (*375 mL*) heavy cream	Combine in heavy saucepan, mixing well, then on medium heat bring to a rolling boil. Now reduce heat (DO NOT STIR!) and cook until mixture reaches 234°F (*112°C*) — soft ball stage.
	Cool to lukewarm (110°F/*34°C*). Now beat until thick. (This will not take very long.)

Spread fudge in an 8″ (*20 cm*) pan and when cool, cut into squares.

Don't be afraid to use a candy thermometer.

Zuccotto Florentino with slivers of white chocolate (page 32)

Chocolate Mousse Trifle

This extraordinary trifle was chosen the Best Tasting Dessert, professional category, at Vancouver's first Chocolate Festival. There are six steps to its preparation:

1 Make the cake a day ahead if possible.
2 Now make the mousse.
3 Then whip the cream and divide it in half.
4 Measure the toasted nuts.
5 Combine milk and liqueur.
6 Assemble and enjoy.

Preheat oven to 325°F (*160°C*).

Chocolate Cake

2 medium eggs 1 cup (*250 mL*) sugar 2 Tbsp. (*30 mL*) soft butter 1 cup (*250 mL*) oil ½ cup (*125 mL*) cocoa, packed ½ cup (*125 mL*) buttermilk 1 tsp. (*5 mL*) vanilla	Combine in this order.
2¼ cups (*550 mL*) flour 1½ tsp. (*7 mL*) baking powder 1½ tsp. (*7 mL*) baking soda	Sift and add to above.
1 cup (*250 mL*) boiling water	Fold in. Then fold mixture into two prepared, round 8″ or 9″ (*20–22 cm*) pans and bake for 25 minutes.

Chocolate Amaretto Mousse

1½ cups (*375 mL*) chocolate chips	Process in food processor for 5 seconds.
3 Tbsp. (*45 mL*) boiling water	Add to chocolate and process until smooth.
4 egg yolks 3 Tbsp. (*45 mL*) soft butter	Add items one at a time to chocolate.

1 Tbsp. (*15 mL*) Amaretto liqueur	
4 egg whites	Beat in a large bowl until soft peaks form, then fold chocolate into egg whites.
	Set aside.

Cream

1 qt. (*1 L*) heavy cream ½ cup (*125 mL*) icing sugar	Beat together until soft peaks form. Divide cream mixture in half.
¼ cup (*50 mL*) cold strong coffee 1 Tbsp. (*15 mL*) instant coffee 1 Tbsp. (*15 mL*) coffee liqueur	Combine, add to one-half of the cream and beat. Then set aside both bowls.

Nuts and Liqueur

1 cup (*250 mL*) toasted nuts	Your favourite: hazelnuts, pecans, almonds or walnuts.
1 cup (*250 mL*) milk ⅓ cup (*75 mL*) coffee or chocolate liqueur	Combine.
1 cup (*250 mL*) Bittersweet Fudge Sauce (page 37)	

To Assemble

In a 4 qt. (*4 L*) glass bowl: Spoon some cream on bottom of bowl; dunk some cake in milk mixture and place over cream. Drizzle on one-third fudge sauce. Sprinkle some nuts on this, then pour half the mousse over the cake. Add more cake and more nuts; then add coffee-flavoured cream and more fudge sauce. Add remaining cake, more nuts, and rest of mousse. Top with remaining cream and fudge sauce and sprinkle with nuts.

A seduction of liqueur-drenched cake and creams. Delightfully decadent.

Homemade Chocolate Mints

Preheat oven to 350°F (*180°C*).

6 oz. (*170 g*) unsweetened chocolate ¾ cup (*175 mL*) butter	In double boiler melt over hot water.
3 eggs 1½ cups (*375 mL*) sugar ½ tsp. (*2 mL*) peppermint extract	In separate bowl beat eggs until frothy. Add sugar, extract and then stir into chocolate mixture.
¾ cup (*175 mL*) flour	Add and mix well.

Pour into buttered 9″ × 13″ (*22 cm × 33 cm*) pan and bake for 20–25 minutes until finger does not leave indent. DO NOT OVERBAKE.

1 cup (*250 mL*) icing sugar 2 Tbsp. (*30 mL*) milk 1 tsp. (*5 mL*) peppermint extract Green food colouring	Mix well and spread over base.
2 oz. (*60 g*) semi-sweet chocolate	Melt and drizzle over mints. Cut into thin bars or squares.

No commercial chocolate mints can match these for richness and flavour. Serve after a meal or on festive occasions. They freeze beautifully.

Tout Sweet Cappuccino Truffles

8 oz. (*250 g*) semi-sweet chocolate 3½ Tbsp. (*50 mL*) butter	Melt and remove from heat. Beat together until blended.
2 tsp. (*10 mL*) instant coffee	Add.
¼ cup (*50 mL*) evaporated milk	Add.
	Chill until set. Roll into balls (makes about 20). Freeze for 1 hour.

4 oz. (*115 g*) white chocolate, melted	Dip frozen truffles into white chocolate. Remove quickly to prevent dark chocolate from melting into white.
	Chill until ready to serve.

Our friend Anna De Flores of Gastown's Tout Sweet is famous for her truffles. She has graciously permitted us to pass on this recipe — our favourite.

Black Bottom Cupcakes

	Preheat oven to 350°F (*180°C*).
¼ cup (*50 mL*) cocoa 1 cup (*250 mL*) sugar 1 tsp. (*5 mL*) baking soda 1½ cups (*375 mL*) flour	Combine in this order.
1 cup (*250 mL*) water ⅓ cup (*75 mL*) light oil 2 Tbsp. (*30 mL*) white vinegar 1 tsp. (*5 mL*) vanilla	Mix together until blended, then slowly add to the above.
	Line cupcake tins with paper containers and fill each two-thirds full.
½ cup (*125 mL*) soft cream cheese 1 egg ¼ cup (*50 mL*) sugar	Blend well and drop by spoonfuls onto chocolate cupcake bases.
1 cup (*250 mL*) chocolate chips	Sprinkle each cupcake with chocolate chips.

Bake for 25 minutes. Yield: one dozen.

A coveted Lazy Gourmet recipe.

Chocolate Chunk Reversals

Preheat oven to 350°F (*180°C*).

⅓ cup (*75 mL*) butter	Cream well.
½ cup (*125 mL*) white sugar	Add gradually.
½ cup (*125 mL*) brown sugar	Add gradually.
1 egg	Add and beat well.
⅔ cup (*150 mL*) flour 2 tsp. (*10 mL*) baking powder ½ cup (*125 mL*) cocoa	Sift together and add one-half flour mixture to above.
⅓ cup (*75 mL*) milk	Add.
	Now add rest of flour mixture.
2 cups (*500 mL*) rolled oats 3½ oz. (*100 g*) white chocolate chunks ½ cups (*125 mL*) raisins	Add and mix well.

Drop by teaspoons onto lightly buttered baking sheet. Bake for 20 minutes. Makes 30 cookies.

An enticing combination of chew and crunch.

PECANS

Frosty Butter Pecan Mousse

	Line a 4 cup (*1 L*) bowl or ring mould with plastic wrap.
2 egg whites ½ cup (*125 mL*) sugar	Using electric mixer, beat egg whites until soft peaks form. Add sugar gradually and beat until stiff peaks form.
2 egg yolks 1 tsp. (*5 mL*) vanilla	Beat well and carefully fold whites into yolks.
1 cup (*250 mL*) heavy cream	Beat until soft peaks form. Fold into egg mixture.
¾ cup (*175 mL*) toasted pecans, coarsely chopped 1½ oz. (*45 g*) unsweetened chocolate, finely chopped	Fold into above.
Hot Fudge Sauce (page 37) (optional)	

Pour into ring mould and freeze until firm. Decorate with whole pecans or pour fudge sauce over mousse just before serving.

A simple extravagance.

Pecan Fudge Cake

	Preheat oven to 325°F (*160°C*).
½ cup (*125 mL*) butter	Cream butter.
1½ cups (*375 mL*) sugar	Gradually add sugar.
6 oz. (*170 g*) unsweetened chocolate, melted and slightly cooled	Slowly add chocolate.
3 eggs	Add eggs one at a time, beating after each addition.
2 cups (*500 mL*) flour 2 tsp. (*10 mL*) baking powder }	Sift together.
1½ cups (*375 mL*) milk 2 tsp. (*10 mL*) vanilla }	Mix together.
	Now add flour and milk alternately to chocolate mixture, starting and ending with flour.
1 cup (*250 mL*) pecans, toasted and chopped	Add.

Pour into three prepared, round 9″ (*22 cm*) pans. Bake for 25 minutes. Ice with Pecan Fudge Icing.

Pecan Fudge Icing

½ cup (*125 mL*) soft butter	Cream.
4 oz. (*115 g*) unsweetened chocolate, melted and slightly cooled	Add.
3 cups (*750 mL*) icing sugar	Add slowly, creaming until smooth.
2 tsp. (*10 mL*) lemon juice 2 tsp. (*10 mL*) vanilla }	Add.

¾ cup (*175 mL*) pecans, toasted and chopped

Stir in nuts.

¼ cup (*50 mL*) pecan halves

Ice between layers and over top and sides, then decorate with pecan halves.

Pecan Glazed Torte

Preheat oven to 350°F (*180°C*).

6 oz. (*170 g*) semi-sweet chocolate

Melt and set aside.

½ cup (*125 mL*) soft butter

Beat until very smooth.

½ cup (*125 mL*) sugar

Gradually add to butter until mixture is fluffy.

4 egg yolks

Beat into butter mixture one at a time.

Add chocolate and blend.

1 cup (*250 mL*) pecans, finely chopped
4 Tbsp. (*60 mL*) flour

Mix and add to above.

4 egg whites

Beat until stiff and gently fold in.

The Lazy Gourmet Glaze (page 13)

Pour into prepared, round 9″ (*22 cm*) pan. Bake for 25 minutes. When cooled, place cake on rack over plate. Pour glaze over cake and tilt cake to edge glaze over sides. Decorate with pecans. Serve chilled.

Although this torte is rich and dense, the lightness of the pecans gives it an almost ethereal quality.

Apple Pecan Kugel

Preheat oven to 350°F (*180°C*).

5 Tbsp. (*75 mL*) melted butter
1 cup (*250 mL*) brown sugar
1 cup (*250 mL*) pecan halves

Mix and press into bottom of tube pan.

1 lb. (*500 g*) fresh fettucine
or 12 oz. (*340 g*) dried fettucine
(flat egg noodles)

Cook fresh fettucine for 5 minutes in boiling water (about 9 minutes for dried fettucine). Drain and rinse with cold water. Set aside.

¾ cup (*175 mL*) sugar
5 eggs
1 cup (*250 mL*) sour cream
1 tsp. (*5 mL*) vanilla

Mix well together and set aside.

2 cups (*500 mL*) apples,
peeled and chopped
1 Tbsp. (*15 mL*) cinnamon
¼ cup (*50 mL*) flour

Combine.

Now mix noodles, apples and egg mixture. Pour into tube pan. Bake for one hour. Let sit for 15 minutes. Invert and serve warm or at room temperature.

Great brunch food or late evening snack. Serve with yogurt or sour cream. Kugel tastes even better reheated.

Lynnie's Pecan Crisp Refrigerator Cookies

¾ cup (*175 mL*) soft butter ⅔ cup (*150 mL*) sugar	Using electric mixer, beat butter for 30 seconds. Gradually add sugar and beat until fluffy.
1 egg 1 tsp. (*5 mL*) vanilla ¼ tsp. (*1 mL*) cinnamon	Add to mixture.
1¾ cups (*425 mL*) flour ¼ tsp. (*1 mL*) salt	Add and roll mixture into three logs.
	Wrap with waxed paper and chill for 30 minutes.
¾ cup (*200 mL*) pecans, chopped	Roll logs in pecans and rewrap. Chill overnight.

Preheat oven to 350°F (*180°C*). Slice dough into ½" (*1 cm*) slices and bake on nonstick or lightly buttered cookie sheet for 10–12 minutes.

Pecan Chip Cookies

Preheat oven to 350°F (*180°C*).

1 cup (*250 mL*) butter	Using electric mixer, cream well.
1 cup (*250 mL*) brown sugar	Add gradually and beat until light and fluffy.

1 egg
1 tsp. (*5 mL*) vanilla } Add.

1½ cups (*375 mL*) flour
1 tsp. (*5 mL*) baking powder } Sift together and add.

½ cup (*125 mL*) pecans, chopped
1 cup (*250 mL*) chocolate chips } Add and mix.

Drop by spoonfuls onto buttered cookie sheet and bake for 10–12 minutes. Makes about 3 dozen.

This is the cookie recipe you've been looking for!

Pecan Shortbread Squares

Preheat oven to 350°F (*180°C*).

1 cup (*250 mL*) butter 6 Tbsp. (*90 mL*) brown sugar 1 egg 1 tsp. (*5 mL*) lemon juice 3 cups (*750 mL*) flour	Blend well with food processor, electric mixer or hands.

Press into 10″ × 15″ (*25 cm* × *29 cm*) pan. Prick with fork. Bake for 20 minutes.

3 cups (*750 mL*) pecans	Spread pecans over shortbread.
¾ cup (*175 mL*) butter 7 Tbsp. (*105 mL*) honey	In heavy saucepan, melt butter and honey together.
¾ cup (*175 mL*) brown sugar	Add and bring to boil, cooking until dark brown, about 5–7 minutes, whisking continuously. Remove from heat.
3 Tbsp. (*45 mL*) heavy cream	Add immediately. Mix and pour over pecans.

Return shortbread to oven for 20 minutes. Cool to room temperature before cutting into squares.

The caramel glues the pecans to the shortbread, creating a new version of an old southern favourite.

Pecan Rum Balls

1½ cups (*375 mL*) graham wafer crumbs
1 cup (*250 mL*) icing sugar
1 cup (*250 mL*) pecans, chopped
2½ Tbsp. (*40 mL*) cocoa
¼ cup (*50 mL*) corn syrup (light or dark)
¼ cup (*50 mL*) dark rum

Mix all ingredients until well blended. (Get your hands in there!)

Icing sugar, cocoa or melted chocolate

Roll into balls, then roll in icing sugar, cocoa *or* dip into melted chocolate. Makes about 3 dozen.

They freeze well. Keep on hand in case of emergency, i.e., guests or chocolate attack.

Diddy's Delights

Preheat oven to 300°F (*150°C*).

1 cup (*250 mL*) soft butter
½ cup (*125 mL*) icing sugar
1½ Tbsp. (*25 mL*) vanilla
1¾ cups (*435 mL*) flour
1 cup (*250 mL*) pecans, finely chopped

Mix together well and drop by teaspoons onto ungreased cookie sheet.

Bake for 25 minutes. When cool, roll in icing sugar.

These freeze well, but don't roll in sugar until thawed. Makes 4 dozen.

The easiest recipe in the book.

Pecan Fudge Pie

Preheat oven to 350°F (*180°C*).

Chocolate Crust (page 24)

Fudge Filling

1¼ cups (*300 mL*) pecan halves	Spread over bottom of unbaked 9″ (*23 cm*) chocolate pie shell.
3 eggs	Beat eggs.
½ cup (*125 mL*) brown sugar ½ cup (*125 mL*) white sugar 1 cup (*250 mL*) light corn syrup	Add to eggs separately, mixing well after each addition.
3 oz. (*85 mL*) unsweetened chocolate ⅓ cup (*75 mL*) butter	Melt together and add.
1 tsp. (*5 mL*) vanilla	Add.

Pour filling into shell and bake for 40 minutes. Chill for 2 hours. Serve with unsweetened whipped cream.

Worth every calorie.

The Lazy Gourmet Pecan Pie

Preheat oven to 350°F (*180°C*).

1 unbaked 9″ (*23 cm*) pie shell
(page 24)

3 eggs	Beat eggs.
1 cup (*250 mL*) brown sugar	Add sugar and mix.
⅓ cup (*75 mL*) melted butter	Stir in.
1 cup (*250 mL*) light corn syrup	Stir in.
½ tsp. (*2 mL*) vanilla	Add.
1⅓ cups (*325 mL*) pecans, toasted	Put pecans in pie shell.
	Pour filling over pecans. (They will rise to the top.)

Bake for 45 minutes. Serve chilled or at room temperature with whipped cream.

We've searched but can find no richer, more satisfying pecan pie recipe. Once you cut into it, you'll want to "even the edges" until it's all gone.

Chocolate Glazed Pecan Pie

Chocolate Crust (page 24)

The Lazy Gourmet Pecan Pie
Filling (page 52)

Pour into crust and refrigerate.
When chilled, spread with
Fudge Glaze.

Fudge Glaze

1 cup (*250 mL*) chocolate chips,
melted and slightly cooled
1 Tbsp. (*15 mL*) brandy
2 Tbsp. (*30 mL*) soft butter

Whisk until well blended.
Spread over pie and decorate
with pecan halves.

Our famous pecan pie filling sandwiched between two layers of chocolate fantasy.

Chocolate Glazed Pecan Pie with Chocolate Crust (page 24)

The Quintessential Turtle

1½ cups (*375 mL*) whole pecans, toasted	Place on buttered cookie sheet in clumps of threes.

Caramel

1 cup (*250 mL*) sugar ⅔ cup (*150 mL*) light corn syrup ⅔ cup (*150 mL*) light cream dash salt 3 Tbsp. (*45 mL*) butter	In medium-sized saucepan, mix well and bring to a boil, stirring constantly.
⅓ cup (*75 mL*) light cream	When mixture starts to boil, add more cream and cook slowly until candy thermometer reads 246°F (*118°C*) (firm ball stage).
½ tsp. (*2 mL*) vanilla	Remove from heat and add vanilla.
	Let cool for one minute. Mix well and, using two teaspoons — one for scooping, one for pushing — drop caramel onto pecans.
	Let harden about 5 minutes.
4 oz. (*115 g*) semi-sweet chocolate, melted	Spread over caramel.

This recipe was donated by a fiendish dentist!

HAZELNUTS

Hazelnut Truffles

6 oz. (*170 g*) chocolate chips,
melted
2 Tbsp. (*30 mL*) brandy
2 Tbsp. (*30 mL*) light corn
syrup
⅔ cup (*150 mL*) icing sugar
½ cup (*125 mL*) hazelnuts,
toasted and crushed

} Mix together and form into balls. Chill well.

4 oz. (*115 g*) semi-sweet
chocolate, melted
⅛ tsp. (*0.5 mL*) paraffin wax
(optional)

} Dip truffles in chocolate *or* roll in sifted cocoa.

or cocoa

So simple, this frequently requested recipe can be prepared in a few minutes.

Hazelnut Brownie Tarte with Raspberry Sauce or Mint Crème

Preheat oven to 350°F (*180°C*).

Pastry

1 cup (*250 mL*) flour ¼ cup (*50 mL*) brown sugar 3 Tbsp. (*45 mL*) cocoa ½ cup (*125 mL*) well-chilled butter 2 Tbsp. (*30 mL*) milk 1 tsp. (*5 mL*) vanilla	Using food processor, or pastry cutter, combine and mix until well blended.
	Press into prepared 11″ (*28 cm*) ring flan pan.

Filling

3 oz. (*85 g*) unsweetened chocolate 3 oz. (*85 g*) semi-sweet chocolate	Melt together in double boiler. Remove from heat.
½ cup (*125 mL*) butter	Add butter 1 Tbsp. (*15 mL*) at a time until blended.
1½ cups (*375 mL*) sugar	Add.
3 eggs, beaten	Add eggs slowly, blending well.
2 tsp. (*10 mL*) vanilla ¾ cups (*175 mL*) hazelnuts, toasted and coarsely chopped	Add vanilla and hazelnuts.
¾ cup (*175 mL*) flour	Add and blend well.

Pour into unbaked tarte shell. Bake for 25–30 minutes, until tooth-pick comes out clean. Be careful not to overbake. Serve with Raspberry or Mint Crème Sauce.

A down-home brownie served with the elegance of a French dessert. To be absolutely outrageous, serve with both sauces, a spoonful on either side of each slice.

Raspberry Sauce

10 oz. (*275 g*) pkg. frozen
raspberries *or* 2 cups (*500 mL*)
fresh raspberries
1 Tbsp. (*15 mL*) kirsch
4 Tbsp. (*60 mL*) sugar

Process in blender or food processor until smooth. If desired, press through sieve to remove seeds.

For a thicker sauce, heat raspberries until mixture boils. Simmer for 30 seconds. Remove from heat and process in blender.

Mint Sauce
(Crème à l'anglaise au Crème de Menthe)

3 cups (*750 mL*) milk

Heat milk in top of double boiler over boiling water until very hot.

5 egg yolks
⅓ cup (*75 mL*) sugar
1½ Tbsp. (*25 mL*) flour

Mix in a bowl.

Add milk to egg mixture, stirring with a wire whisk. Return to top of double boiler and cook over simmering water until thickened, stirring constantly.

Cool by placing pot in cold water.

3½ Tbsp. (*75 mL*) crème
de menthe
1 tsp. (*5 mL*) peppermint
extract

Add flavourings.

Frozen Hazelnut Soufflé

Prepare 8″, 2 qt. (*20 cm, 2 L*) soufflé dish. Make a collar by cutting a piece of foil long enough to overlap around dish. Oil the part that will be inside. The foil should extend 4″ (*10 cm*) above edge of dish.

1¾ cups (*425 mL*) sugar
1 cup (*250 mL*) water

Stir together in small saucepan. Let boil without stirring for 5 minutes.

9 egg yolks

Beat with electric mixer (using large bowl) at medium speed until lemon coloured.

Increase speed to high and slowly add sugar syrup. Continue to beat until cool and stiff.

3 cups (*750 mL*) heavy cream

Beat until stiff, then fold all but ½ cup (*125 mL*) into egg mixture.

1 cup (*250 mL*) hazelnuts, toasted and chopped
4 Tbsp. (*60 mL*) Frangelico liqueur

Add.

Spoon into soufflé dish. Decorate with remaining whipped cream. Freeze for 6–8 hours or overnight. Serve while frozen.

Serious competition for the best ice cream you've ever had and *you don't need an ice cream maker.*

Chocolate Frangelico Cheesecake

Preheat oven to 350°F (*180°C*).

Chocolate Crust (page 24)   Press into 9″ or 10″ (*23–26 cm*) springform pan.

Filling

2 cups (*500 mL*) soft cream cheese
½ cup (*125 mL*) sugar
4 oz. (*115 g*) semi-sweet chocolate, melted and slightly cooled
1 oz. (*30 g*) unsweetened chocolate, melted and slightly cooled
2 large eggs
½ cup (*125 mL*) sour cream
2 Tbsp. (*30 mL*) Frangelico liqueur
3 Tbsp. (*45 mL*) hazelnut purée (optional)

Beat with electric mixer, adding ingredients in this order and then beating for 10 minutes on medium-high speed.

Pour over crust and bake for 30–35 minutes until firm to touch. Cool, then chill 2–3 hours.

Topping

1 cup (*250 mL*) heavy cream   Beat until *soft* peaks form.

2 Tbsp. (*30 mL*) icing sugar
2 Tbsp. (*30 mL*) Frangelico liqueur
Combine and spread over cake.

4 Tbsp. (*60 mL*) hazelnuts, toasted and crushed
chocolate curls
Decorate with crushed nuts and chocolate curls (page 5).

The current number one cheesecake at The Lazy Gourmet. Decorative curls made with Belgian hazelnut chocolate are easier to work with than regular chocolate.

Dacquoise

Preheat oven to 350°F (*180°C*).

Cake

| 2 Tbsp. (*30 mL*) butter | Melt and cool butter. Set aside. |

⅓ cup (*75 mL*) sugar
4 egg yolks
1 tsp. (*5 mL*) vanilla
1 tsp. (*5 mL*) Cointreau
} Beat together until very light and fluffy. Set aside.

4 egg whites
pinch of salt
} Using electric mixer, beat until soft peaks form.

⅓ cup (*75 mL*) sugar — Add to egg whites, 1 Tbsp. (*15 mL*) at a time, beating until stiff but not dry. Set aside.

½ cup (*125 mL*) flour
⅓ cup (*75mL*) cornstarch
} Sift together.

Add one-third whites to yolks, then sift one-half flour over mixture; add another one-third whites, then rest of flour, ending with whites. Now gently fold in the butter.

Pour into two prepared, round 9″ (*22 cm*) pans and set aside.

¼ cup (*50 mL*) hazelnuts, toasted and crushed
¼ cup (*50 mL*) sugar
⅓ cup (*75 mL*) cornstarch
} Mix together and set aside.

3 egg whites
⅛ tsp. (*0.5 mL*) cream of tartar

} Beat whites and cream of tartar until soft peaks form.

½ cup (*125 mL*) sugar
½ tsp. (*2 mL*) vanilla

Gradually add sugar, then vanilla.

Now carefully fold nut mixture into egg whites.

Using pastry bag and largest tip, pipe meringue over both layers.

Chocolate Buttercream
(page 64)

Bake for 35 minutes. Cool. Fill and frost with Chocolate Buttercream.

An explosion of textures and flavours.

Chocolate Buttercream

1 cup (*250 mL*) sugar ⅓ cup (*75 mL*) water	Combine in small heavy saucepan, cover and bring to boil. Boil for 2 minutes and remove cover. Boil to 240°F (*112°C*) — soft ball stage.
8 egg yolks	In bowl, using electric mixer, beat yolks on high speed until thick.
	Reduce speed to medium and gradually pour in hot syrup.
	Return to high speed and beat until mixture is cool.
1½ cups (*375 mL*) soft unsalted butter	Begin adding, 1 Tbsp. (*15 mL*) at a time until all butter is added.
6 oz. (*170 mL*) unsweetened chocolate, melted and slightly cooled 1 tsp. (*5 mL*) vanilla	Add chocolate and vanilla.

Hazelnut Torte

	Preheat oven to 350°F (*180°C*).
7 egg whites	In large bowl, beat until frothy.
⅓ cup (*75 mL*) sugar	Add very slowly to egg whites, beating until stiff peaks form.
7 egg yolks	In another bowl, beat until very light.
⅓ cup (*75 mL*) sugar 1 tsp. (*5 mL*) vanilla	Add to yolks and beat until thick and lemon coloured.
1¼ cups (*300 mL*) hazelnuts, toasted and ground 3 Tbsp. (*45 mL*) graham cracker crumbs 1 tsp. (*5 mL*) baking powder dash of salt	Combine and fold into yolks.
	Add yolk mixture to whites.
	Pour into three round 8″ or 9″ (*20–22 cm*) pans which have been lined with waxed paper *or* onto a waxed paper-lined 10″ × 15″ (*26 cm × 29 cm*) sheet.

Bake for 15–18 minutes or until cake springs back when lightly touched. Be careful not to overcook. Cool. (If cookie sheet is used, cut into three equal pieces.)

Incredible Chocolate Icing
(page 11) *or* Chocolate
Buttercream (page 64)

Fill with flavoured whipped cream and ice with Incredible Chocolate Icing. Or, for an extra indulgence, fill and ice with Chocolate Buttercream. Chill for at least one hour. Use serrated knife to cut.

Hazelnut Fudge Torte

Preheat oven to 350°F (180°C).

⅔ cup (*150 mL*) hazelnuts, toasted and ground
¼ cup (*50 mL*) flour
1½ Tbsp. (*25 mL*) ground coffee beans
} Combine and set aside.

1 cup (*250 mL*) butter
7 oz. (*200 g*) semi-sweet chocolate
¾ cup (*175 mL*) sugar
} Melt butter and chocolate and let cool for a couple of minutes, then add sugar.

1½ Tbsp. (*25 mL*) coffee liqueur
4 eggs
} Mix well and add to chocolate mixture.

Now add dry ingredients.

Bake in prepared, round 9″ (*22 cm*) pan (or springform pan) for 25 minutes. Do not overbake. Cool, then chill.

The Lazy Gourmet Glaze
(page 13)

Place cake on rack with plate underneath. Pour glaze over top and gently spoon over sides. Decorate with 8–10 whole hazelnuts, toasted.

This torte is best when chilled for a couple of days. It freezes well, so that you can make it ahead and glaze it the day you serve it.

Raspberry Hazelnut Meringue Squares

Preheat oven to 350°F (*180°C*).

Base

½ cup (*125 mL*) soft butter	Cream.
½ cup (*125 mL*) icing sugar	Add to butter.
2 egg yolks	Stir in yolks, one at a time.
1¼ cups (*300 mL*) flour	Add flour.

Press mixture into buttered 9″ (*22 cm*) square pan, prick with fork and bake for 15–18 minutes. Cool for 5 minutes.

¾ cup (*175 mL*) raspberry jam or preserves	Spread over base.

Meringue Topping

2 egg whites pinch salt pinch cream of tartar ½ cup (*125 mL*) sugar	Beat whites with salt and cream of tartar until peaks form. Gradually add sugar and beat until mixture is glossy and forms stiff peaks.
1 cup (*250 mL*) hazelnuts, toasted and ground ½ tsp. (*2 mL*) vanilla	Fold in hazelnuts and vanilla.

Carefully spread meringue over jam and bake at 350°F (*180°C*) for 25–30 minutes until top is lightly browned. Drizzle 2 oz. (*60 g*) melted semi-sweet chocolate over top. Cool before cutting.

ALMONDS

Chocolate Almond Gateau

	Preheat oven to 350°F (*180°C*).
1 cup (*250 mL*) soft butter	Cream.
1 cup (*250 mL*) sugar	Add gradually.
5 egg yolks	Beat in one at a time.
4 oz. (*115 g*) semi-sweet chocolate 4 oz. (*115 g*) unsweetened chocolate	Melt chocolate; let cool and pour into yolk mixture.
1 cup (*250 mL*) flour 6 Tbsp. (*90 mL*) milk	Add flour and milk alternately, stirring after each addition.
1 tsp. (*5 mL*) vanilla 2 tsp. (*10 mL*) Amaretto liqueur	Stir in.
1½ cups (*375 mL*) almonds, toasted and ground	Add.
5 egg whites	Beat until stiff peaks form. Fold one-third egg white mixture into chocolate, then gently fold in the rest.

Pour into shallow round 14″ (*38 cm*) pan lined with waxed paper. Bake for 25 minutes. Top should be firm when touched. But don't overbake! Remove carefully from oven and chill 2–3 hours before icing.

Truffle Icing Glaze

8 oz. (*225 g*) semi-sweet chocolate
6 Tbsp. (*90 mL*) milk
6 Tbsp. (*90 mL*) butter
} Melt in top of double boiler and let cool slightly.

1¾ cups (*425 mL*) icing sugar, sifted
½ tsp. (*2 mL*) almond extract
2 tsp. (*10 mL*) Amaretto liqueur
} Beat into chocolate mixture.

Gently spread over top and sides of gateau. Decorate with slivered toasted almonds.

A gateau to die for. Choose your dinner guests carefully.

Amaretto Cheesecake

Preheat oven to 350°F (*180°C*).

Graham Cracker Crust

1⅓ cups (*325 mL*) graham cracker crumbs
⅓ cup (*75 mL*) melted butter
¼ cup (*50 mL*) crushed almonds (untoasted)
¼ cup (*50 mL*) brown sugar

Mix to blend well and press into 9" (*23 cm*) springform pan.

Bake for 5 minutes. Remove from oven.

2 cups (*500 mL*) soft cream cheese — Cream well.

½ cup (*125 mL*) sour cream — Add and blend.
⅔ cup (*150 mL*) sugar — Add and blend.
3 medium eggs — Beat in one at a time.

1 Tbsp. (*15 mL*) almond extract
1 Tbsp. (*15 mL*) Amaretto liqueur

Add.

Beat mixture until smooth.

Pour over crust. Bake for 30–35 minutes. Let sit for 5 minutes and then put on topping.

Topping

1 cup (*250 mL*) sour cream
2 Tbsp. (*30 mL*) sugar
2 Tbsp. (*30 mL*) Amaretto liqueur

Mix and smooth gently over cheesecake.

5 Tbsp. (*75 mL*) flaked almonds, toasted

Sprinkle over cheesecake and return to oven for 5 minutes.

Let reach room temperature, then chill for 3–4 hours.

You may want to rename this cheesecake Amoretto *and seduce your favourite victim.*

Unbelievable Chocolate Mousse (page 13), White Chocolate Mousse (page 19), Tout Sweet Cappuccino Trufflles (page 40), Hazelnut Truffles (page 57)

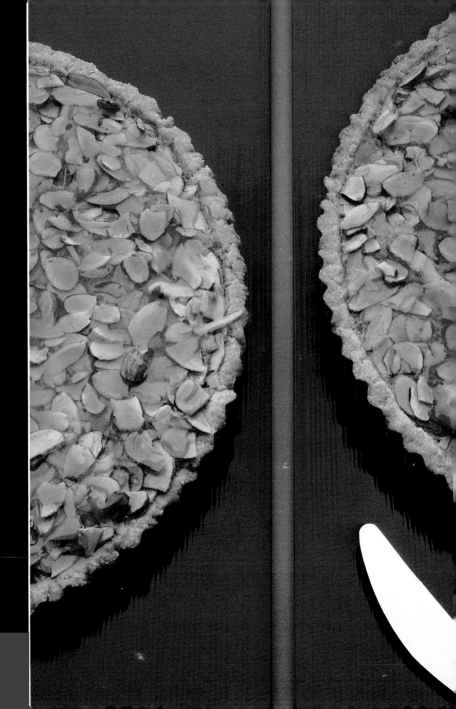

Almond Glazed Tarte

Preheat oven to 350°F (*180°C*).

2 cups (*500 mL*) flour
½ cup (*125 mL*) sugar
½ cup (*125 mL*) butter

Process in food processor until coarse (or blend using pastry blender).

2 eggs
½ tsp. (*2 mL*) vanilla
½ tsp. (*2 mL*) lemon juice

Beat together, then add to processor and continue to mix until ball forms (or mix until well blended).

Press into 11″ (*28 cm*) ring flan pan. Prick all over with fork. Set aside.

½ cup (*125 mL*) butter
⅔ cup (*150 mL*) sugar

Melt butter.
Add sugar.

3 eggs, beaten
1⅓ cups (*325 mL*) blanched almonds, ground
1 Tbsp. (*15 mL*) Amaretto liqueur

Add eggs, then nuts and liqueur.

Pour mixture carefully over crust.

1 cup (*250 mL*) flaked almonds

Gently sprinkle over top so that entire surface is covered. Bake for 35 minutes.

½ cup (*125 mL*) apricot jam
2 Tbsp. (*30 mL*) water

Heat and gently brush over tarte while still warm.

For those who enjoy a European marzipan-like dessert. Makes a lovely presentation for the afternoon tea table.

Almond Glazed Tarte

Almond Mocha Torte

Preheat oven to 350°F (*180°C*).

Genoise

8 egg whites	Beat until soft peaks form.
½ cup (*125 mL*) sugar	Gradually add to egg whites and beat until stiff.
½ tsp. (*2 mL*) almond extract 1 tsp. (*5 mL*) Amaretto liqueur 8 egg yolks, beaten	Beat well and add to whites.
¾ cup (*75 mL*) blanched almonds, ground ½ cup (*125 mL*) flour	Combine and gently fold into egg mixture, one-quarter at a time.
⅓ cup (*75 mL*) butter, clarified and cooled	Gently fold in.

Pour into three prepared, round 8″ or 9″ (*20–22 cm*) pans and bake for 20 minutes until the genoise springs back when touched. Cool slightly before filling and frosting with Mocha Cream.

Mocha Cream

3 oz. (*85 g*) unsweetened chocolate ⅓ cup (*75 mL*) strong coffee 3 Tbsp. (*45 mL*) instant coffee	Melt together over low heat, then cool to room temperature. Set aside.
1½ cups (*375 mL*) soft butter	With electric mixer cream until light.
2 cups (*500 mL*) icing sugar	Add gradually.
3 egg yolks	Beat in one at a time.
1 Tbsp. (*15 mL*) coffee liqueur 1 tsp. (*5 mL*) vanilla	Add to egg mixture, then add all to chocolate mixture. Beat until fluffy.
	Spread over each layer of genoise, and frost top and sides.

Strasbourg Apple Almond Pie

Preheat oven to 375°F (*190°C*).

1 unbaked 9" (*23 cm*) pie shell

4–5 tart apples, peeled and sliced	Place in bowl.
2 Tbsp. (*30 mL*) sugar 1 tsp. (*5 mL*) cinnamon Touch of nutmeg ½ cup (*125 mL*) toasted almonds, coarsely chopped	Toss with apples.

Place in unbaked pie shell and bake for 25 minutes.

4 egg yolks ¼ cup (*50 mL*) sugar ¼ cup (*50 mL*) light cream ¼ cup (*50 mL*) heavy cream	Mix together and pour over apples.

Return to oven for 25–30 minutes until golden brown and inserted knife comes out clean.

Apple pie 1980s style!

Lemon Mousse Tarte
in Almond Crust

Preheat oven to 400°F (*200°C*).

Pastry

1½ cups (*375 mL*) flour ½ cup (*125 mL*) sugar grated peel of 1 lemon 4 Tbsp. (*60 mL*) almonds, ground	Place in food processor and process for 3 seconds.
⅓ cup (*75 mL*) cold butter	Add and process until coarse.
1 egg 1 Tbsp. (*15 mL*) lemon juice	Add and process until ball forms.
	Press into ring flan pan. Chill.

Prick with fork. Bake for 20–25 minutes, until golden brown. Cool.

Mousse

3 eggs 3 egg yolks ⅔ cup (*150 mL*) lemon juice ¾ cup (*175 mL*) sugar	Mix in top part of double boiler. Beat well with stainless steel wire whisk. Place over simmering water and whisk until thickened (about 10 minutes).
	Let cool. Whisk slightly, then pour into pastry shell.
	Chill.

Glaze

¾ cup (*175 mL*) water ½ cup (*125 mL*) sugar	Combine in small saucepan. Bring to a boil and boil until the thermometer reads 220°F (*105°C*).

2 Tbsp. (*30 mL*) lemon juice	Add lemon juice and boil until mixture reaches 240°F (*115°C*).
	Gently brush over mousse. Serve with raspberry sauce (page 59).

Occasionally, this delicious mousse will crack. Don't despair. Just smother with raspberry sauce and no one will notice.

Chocolate Florentines

Preheat oven to 325°F (*160°C*).

½ cup (*125 mL*) butter ¼ cup (*50 mL*) honey ¼ cup (*50 mL*) light corn syrup	Place in saucepan and bring to a boil; remove from heat and let cool.
1 cup (*250 mL*) flour 1 cup (*250 mL*) almonds, finely chopped 2 tsp. (*10 mL*) brandy ½ tsp. (*2 mL*) ground ginger	Add and mix well.

Drop by ½ tsp. (*2 mL*) at least 3″ (*8 cm*) apart onto nonstick or greased cookie sheets. Bake for 12–15 minutes. After about one minute, transfer carefully to cooling rack and let cool completely.

3 oz. (*85 g*) semi-sweet chocolate, melted and slightly cooled	Spread a thin layer of chocolate on a cookie and sandwich with another.

When all are sandwiched, chill until set, then store in airtight containers in a cool, dry place. Makes about 2 dozen.

Also known as French lace cookies and usually found only in expensive patisseries.

Praline Custard Parfaits

Praline Powder

⅓ cup (75 mL) flaked almonds, toasted	Place toasted almonds in a buttered pan.
⅓ cup (75 mL) sugar water	Place sugar in small saucepan. Pour in just enough water to cover sugar. Heat, then let boil until sugar turns brown (caramel colour). Pour over nuts. Let sit.

When hardened, crack into pieces, put in blender or processor and process until powdery. (Very easy and lots of fun.)

Custard

6 egg yolks ⅓ cup (75 mL) icing sugar ½ cup (125 mL) Amaretto liqueur ¼ cup (50 mL) orange juice	Place in top part of double boiler over boiling water. Beat until thick.
	Remove from heat and whip until cool.
1 cup (250 mL) heavy cream	Whip until stiff. Fold into custard.
Praline powder	Fold in praline powder.

Pour into individual glass sherbert dishes. Chill 3–4 hours before serving. Even better the next day!

Creamy rich with the flavour of real French praline.

Aunt Martha's Almond Crescent Cookies

Preheat oven to 325°F (*160°C*).

½ cup (*125 mL*) soft butter
⅓ cup (*75 mL*) icing sugar
} Cream together.

1 cup (*250 mL*) flour
½ cup (*125 mL*) ground almonds
} Add and mix well.

Chill for ½ hour. Shape into crescents and flatten slightly.

Place on buttered cookie sheet and bake for 20 minutes. Cool.

3 oz. (*85 g*) semi-sweet chocolate, melted (optional)

Dip half of each crescent into chocolate if desired.
Yields 3 dozen.

They really do melt in your mouth.

Amaretti

Preheat oven to 350°F (*180°C*).

8 oz. (*225 g*) blanched almonds, toasted	Chop fine. (A processor makes this task easy.)
2 egg whites pinch of salt	Beat until soft peaks form.
½ cup (*125 mL*) icing sugar ¼ cup (*50 mL*) sugar	Combine well and add a little at a time to egg whites. Beat mixture until stiff.
¼ tsp. (*1 mL*) almond extract	Add.
	Now fold in almonds.
	Drop batter by teaspoon onto prepared cookie sheet, or pipe with pastry bag, using star tip.
1 cup (*250 mL*) pinenuts *or* 1 cup (*250 mL*) whole almonds	Sprinkle with pinenuts *or* press one almond into the middle of each cookie.

Bake for 15 minutes until lightly browned. Cool and store in airtight containers. Makes about 3 dozen.

The classic Italian almond cookie.

Ss and Ds

	Batter should be prepared the day before.
1 cup (*250 mL*) soft butter	Cream well.
1 cup (*250 mL*) sugar	Add a little at a time, continuing to cream.
4 eggs	Add one at a time and beat well.
1 tsp (*5 mL*) vanilla	Add.
3½ cups (*875 mL*) flour 1 Tbsp. (*15 mL*) baking powder 2 tsp. (*10 mL*) cinnamon 1 cup (*250 mL*) ground almonds	Sift together and add with almonds to batter.
	Refrigerate overnight. Preheat oven to 350°F (*180°C*).
2 cups (*500 mL*) ground almonds 2 cups (*500 mL*) sugar 4 tsp. (*20 mL*) cinnamon	Mix together.

Pinch off a little piece of batter at a time. Roll in nut mixture, working nuts into batter. Form into letters or shapes and place on buttered cookie sheet. Bake for 15–20 minutes until golden. But watch carefully — they can quickly get too dark. Fills six cookie sheets.

Grandma Faye's original Ss and Os.

Chocolate Almond Pretzels

Preheat oven to 350°F (*180°C*).

1 cup (*250 mL*) soft butter 1 cup (*250 mL*) sugar 3 egg yolks 1 cup (*250 mL*) ground almonds 2¼ cups (*550 mL*) flour	Blend well, adding ingredients in the order given.

Break dough into pieces and roll between palms of hands. Form into pretzels or any shape you like. Place on prepared cookie sheet and bake for 15–20 minutes.

4 oz. (*115 g*) semi-sweet chocolate, melted and slightly cooled 2 Tbsp. (*30 mL*) icing sugar ¼ cup (*50 mL*) light cream	Combine and glaze each pretzel carefully.

Makes about 2 dozen.

An easily moulded cookie. We've made these into many different shapes, from Valentine's Day hearts to people's names.

Almond Brie

Preheat oven to 375°F (*190°C*).

2 lb. (*1 kg*) whole round Brie	
3 egg whites	Mix together with fork.
3 Tbsp. (*45 mL*) sugar	Add to egg whites.
2 cups (*500 mL*) flaked almonds, toasted	Gently fold in.

| 3 egg yolks | Place Brie on ungreased baking sheet. Beat yolks together and brush over top and sides of cheese. |

Gently press nut mixture onto top and sides of cheese.

Bake for 20 minutes. Cool for 45 minutes before serving.

An elegant non-sweet to be served with crackers.

The Lazy Gourmet Lemon Squares

Preheat oven to 350°F (*180°C*).

Almond Crust

| 1 cup (*250 mL*) butter ⅓ cup (*75 mL*) sugar 1¾ cups (*425 mL*) flour ½ cup (*125 mL*) almonds, crushed | Combine until crumbly and press into bottom of 9″ × 13″ (*22 cm × 33 cm*) pan. |

Bake for 20 minutes until light brown.

Lemon Filling

| 4 eggs ⅓ cup (*75 mL*) lemon juice 1¼ cups (*300 mL*) sugar | Mix together well. |
| ⅓ cup (*75 mL*) flour 1 tsp. (*5 mL*) baking powder | Sift together, add to filling and mix well. |

Gently spread mixture over crust and bake for 25 minutes. Cool before cutting. Be careful not to overbake.

Cinnamon Almond Shortbread

Preheat oven to 350°F (*180°C*).

1 cup (*250 mL*) sugar 1 cup (*250 mL*) butter	Cream well.
1 Tbsp. (*15 mL*) cinnamon 1 tsp. (*5 mL*) vanilla 1 cup (*250 mL*) almonds, ground	Mix and add.
1 egg yolk	Add and mix.
2 cups (*500 mL*) flour	Add and mix well.
	Press onto a cookie sheet.
1 Tbsp. (*15 mL*) icing sugar	Sprinkle on shortbread.
1 egg white	Whisk, then spread over shortbread with pastry brush.
1 cup (*250 mL*) almonds, ground	Sprinkle over shortbread.
1 Tbsp. (*15 mL*) cinnamon	Sprinkle cinnamon on top.

Bake for 25 minutes. Cut into squares and separate. Return to warm oven for 25–30 minutes to dry out.

Deborah's downfall!

Toasted Almond Buttercrunch

	Preheat oven to 325°F (*160°C*).
½ cup (*125 mL*) butter	Cream until light.
¼ cup (*50 mL*) brown sugar ¼ cup (*50 mL*) white sugar ½ cup (*125 mL*) flour	Add one at a time, beating well after each addition.
¾ cup (*175 mL*) almonds, toasted and chopped	Stir in.
	Press into bottom and along sides of small loaf pan.
½ cup (*125 mL*) butter ¾ cup (*175 mL*) cream cheese }	Using electric mixer, cream together.
⅔ cup (*150 mL*) sugar	Add gradually.
3 eggs	Beat in one at a time.
1¼ cup (*300 mL*) flour ½ tsp. baking powder }	Sift and stir in.
1 tsp. (*5 mL*) vanilla	Add and mix well.
	Pour into crust.

Bake for 50–60 minutes until golden and knife inserted in centre comes out clean.

A delicious pound cake coated with candied almonds that can stand on its own — if it survives the prebaking crust-snitchers.

WALNUTS

New York Blondies

Preheat oven to 350°F (*180°C*).

1 cup (*250 mL*) butter	Melt.
2 cups (*500 mL*) brown sugar	Add and mix well.
4 eggs	Beat in, one at a time.
1½ cups (*375 mL*) flour 2 tsp. (*10 mL*) baking powder	Sift and add all at once.
1½ cups (*375 mL*) chocolate chips 1 cup (*250 mL*) walnuts, chopped	Mix together and add.
2 tsp. (*10 mL*) vanilla	Add.
	Pour dough into prepared 9″ × 13″ (*22 cm × 33 cm*) pan.
¼ cup (*50 mL*) walnuts ¼ cup (*50 mL*) chocolate chips	Mix together and sprinkle over top.
	Bake for 30 minutes.

A popular New York treat. When you wish you were in the Big Apple, bake up a batch.

Grandma's Sour Cream Coffee Cake

Preheat oven to 350°F (*180°C*).

1 cup (*250 mL*) soft butter	Cream well.
1 cup (*250 mL*) sugar	Add gradually.
3 eggs	Add eggs, one at a time, mixing well after each addition.

1 cup (*250 mL*) sour cream
1 tsp. (*5 mL*) lemon extract } Add to above.

3 cups (*750 mL*) flour
3 tsp. (*15 mL*) baking powder } Sift well and add.
½ tsp. (*2 mL*) baking soda

Place half the batter in 9″ (*22 cm*) prepared springform pan.

Centre and Topping

1 cup (*250 mL*) brown sugar
3 Tbsp. (*45 mL*) cinnamon
¾ cup (*175 mL*) walnuts,
chopped
¾ cup (*175 mL*) chocolate chips
or 4 oz. (*115 g*) semi-sweet
chocolate, grated
} Mix all ingredients together. Sprinkle cake with half the chocolate nut mixture. Cover with rest of batter. Sprinkle with remainder of mixture.

Bake for 50–60 minutes until done.

Lynnie's Baklava

Preheat oven to 350°F (*180°C*).

1½ cups (*375 mL*) walnuts, ground 2 tsp. (*10 mL*) cinnamon 2 Tbsp. (*30 mL*) icing sugar	Mix together.
1 cup (*250 mL*) butter	Melt butter.
½ lb. (*250 g*) filo	Layer filo in 9″ × 13″ (*22 cm × 33 cm*) baking pan (preferably stainless steel or glass), brushing every sheet with melted butter. Sprinkle nut mixture on every third sheet.
	With a sharp knife, score into squares or diamond shapes and bake for 30 minutes.

Syrup

½ cup (*125 mL*) honey ¾ cup (*175 mL*) water 1¼ cups (*300 mL*) sugar Juice of ½ lemon 1 cinnamon stick	Mix together and bring to boil. Boil for 10 minutes, then simmer 10 minutes longer.
	Cool, then pour over filo. Let sit 2–3 hours or overnight. DO NOT REFRIGERATE. Cut completely through to serve.

Can you believe how easy this is?!

Lynnie's Baklava (page 88) and Frozen Hazelnut Soufflé (page 60)

Money-Back Guarantee Brownies

	Preheat oven to 350°F (*180°C*).
1 cup (*250 mL*) butter	Melt butter.
1 cup (*250 mL*) white sugar 1 cup (*250 mL*) brown sugar ¾ cup (*175 mL*) cocoa	Add and blend well.
3 large eggs	Beat in, one at a time.
1 cup (*250 mL*) flour 1½ tsp. (*7 mL*) baking powder	Sift into mixture and stir.
1½ tsp. (*7 mL*) vanilla 1 cup (*250 mL*) walnuts, chopped	Add.
Incredible Chocolate Icing (page 11)	

Pour into prepared 9″ × 13″ (*22 cm × 33 cm*) pan. Bake for 30 minutes. (Centre will be firm but not hard.) Ice when cool.

At the Lazy Gourmet we offer a money-back guarantee if these are not the best brownies you've ever tasted!

Money-Back Guarantee Brownies (page 91) with Incredible Chocolate Icing (page 11), Homemade Chocolate Mints (page 40), Pecan Shortbread Squares (page 49), Diddy's Delights (page 50)

Walnut Fudge Flan

Preheat oven to 350°F (*180°C*).

Shortbread Flan Crust

¾ cup (*175 mL*) butter
1½ cups (*375 mL*) flour
3 Tbsp. (*45 mL*) sugar

Using food processor, process until crumbly.

1½ Tbsp. (*25 mL*) lemon juice

Add juice and process until mixture forms a ball.
or
Cut dry ingredients with pastry blender and add juice.

Press into bottom and sides of a ring flan pan and bake for 15 minutes.

1 cup (*250 mL*) sugar
3 eggs
⅓ cup (*75 mL*) melted butter
½ tsp. (*2 mL*) vanilla
3½ cups (*875 mL*) walnuts, crushed

Mix well, pour over crust and bake for 25–30 minutes or more. Chill.

Glaze

1 cup (*250 mL*) chocolate chips
3 Tbsp. (*45 mL*) butter
1 tsp. (*5 mL*) vanilla

Melt chips.
Add butter and blend.
Add vanilla.
Spread over flan.

Makes 15 spectacular slices. This flan can do nothing to hide its richness.

Maple Walnut Cheesecake

Preheat oven to 350°F (*180°C*).

Crust

1⅓ cups (*325 mL*) graham wafer crumbs

Place in bowl.

⅓ cup (*75 mL*) melted butter
3 Tbsp. (*45 mL*) walnuts, ground
3 Tbsp. (*45 mL*) maple syrup

Mix well and add to crumbs.

Press into 9″ (*22 cm*) prepared springform pan. Bake for 5 minutes.

Centre

2 cups (*500 mL*) soft cream cheese
½ cup (*125 mL*) sour cream
⅓ cup (*75 mL*) sugar
⅓ cup (*75 mL*) maple syrup
1 tsp. (*5 mL*) vanilla
3 eggs

Combine and beat until light. Pour over crust.

Return to oven for 35–40 minutes.

Topping

1 cup (*250 mL*) sour cream
3 Tbsp. (*45 mL*) maple syrup

Mix and gently spread over cake.

4 Tbsp. (*60 mL*) walnuts, toasted

Sprinkle over cake and return to oven for 5 minutes.

Chill 3–4 hours before serving.

The lightest of our cheesecakes.

Chocolate Walnut Bundt Tunnel Cake

Preheat oven to 350°F (*180°C*).

1 cup (*250 mL*) soft butter 1½ cups (*375 mL*) sugar	Beat until light. Add sugar and cream well.
2 egg yolks 2 eggs 2 tsp. (*10 mL*) vanilla	Beat together and add.
2½ cups (*625 mL*) flour 2 tsp. (*10 mL*) baking powder	Sift together and add.
	Pour three-quarters of batter into prepared bundt pan and make a groove through it with the back of a spoon.
1½ cups (*375 mL*) brown sugar 4 Tbsp. (*60 mL*) cocoa 1 tsp. (*5 mL*) vanilla ½ cup (*125 mL*) walnuts, finely chopped 1 cup (*250 mL*) chocolate chips	Combine all ingredients.
2 egg whites	Beat until stiff and fold into above mixture.
	Fill groove with chocolate mixture. Cover with remaining batter. Bake 60–70 minutes.

No need to ice. An exquisite crust invites nibbling.

Italian Cream Cake

	Preheat oven to 350°F (*180°C*).
1 cup (*250 mL*) butter	Cream well.
2 cups (*500 mL*) sugar	Add gradually.
5 egg yolks	Add and mix well.
1 cup (*250 mL*) buttermilk 1 tsp. (*5 mL*) baking soda }	Combine.
2 cups (*500 mL*) flour	Add alternately with buttermilk mixture to egg mixture.
1 cup (*250 mL*) threaded coconut 1 cup (*250 mL*) walnuts, chopped 1 tsp. (*5 mL*) vanilla }	Add.
5 egg whites	Beat until stiff and fold into mixture.

Pour into two prepared, round 9" (*22 cm*) pans and bake for 25 minutes. Ice with Italian Cream Icing.

Italian Cream Icing

½ cup (*125 mL*) soft butter ½ cup (*125 mL*) soft cream cheese 4 Tbsp. (*60 mL*) Amaretto liqueur 3½ cups (*875 mL*) icing sugar }	Beat together well until light and fluffy.
	Fill and spread over top and sides of cake.
2 cups (*500 mL*) long threaded coconut, toasted	To toast coconut, spread on cookie sheet and place in 350°F (*180°C*) oven until light brown.
	Decorate top and sides of cake with coconut.

Walnut Dream Bars

Preheat oven to 325°F (*160°C*).

½ cup (*125 mL*) butter
3 Tbsp. (*45 mL*) brown sugar
1 cup (*250 mL*) flour

Mix well and press into an 8″ (*20 cm*) square pan.

Bake for 15 minutes.

2 eggs
1 cup (*250 mL*) brown sugar
½ tsp. (*2 mL*) baking powder
2 Tbsp. (*30 mL*) flour
1 tsp. (*5 mL*) vanilla
¾ cup (*175 mL*) walnuts, chopped
½ cup (*125 mL*) long threaded coconut

Mix well and pour over crust.

Bake for 20 minutes longer.
Cool before cutting.

Sweet and gooey. A perfect antidote for exercise.

Oatmeal Chocolate Chip Squares

Preheat oven to 350°F (*180°C*).

1¾ cups (*425 mL*) boiling water
1¾ cups (*425 mL*) oatmeal

Combine and let stand for 10 minutes.

3½ Tbsp. (*55 mL*) butter
1½ cups (*375 mL*) white sugar
1¼ cups (*300 mL*) light brown sugar

Add to above and stir until butter melts.

2 large eggs

Add and mix well.

1¾ cups (*435 mL*) flour
3 Tbsp. (*45 mL*) cocoa   } Sift and add to above.
1½ tsp. (*7 mL*) baking soda

Let cool.

5 oz. (*140 g*) small chocolate   Add to cooled batter.
chips

2 oz. (*60 g*) chocolate chips

Pour batter into prepared 9″ × 13″ (*22 cm* × *33 cm*) pan. Sprinkle top with chips and bake for 40 minutes.

A delicious lunchbox treat.

Walnut Chip Banana Bread

Preheat oven to 350°F (*180°C*).

2 large ripe bananas, mashed
1 cup (*250 mL*) sugar   } Combine and mix well.
2 eggs
½ cup (*125 mL*) oil

1¼ cups (*300 mL*) flour   } Sift and mix in.
1 tsp. (*5 mL*) baking soda

½ cup (*125 mL*) walnuts,
chopped   } Add.
½ cup (*125 mL*) chocolate chips

or 2 oz. (*60 g*) semi-sweet
chocolate, chopped fine

Pour into buttered loaf pan. Bake for 1 hour until loaf springs back when touched.

This bread freezes well and stays fresh when refrigerated. You'll never find a better banana bread recipe!

PEANUTS

Peanut Caramel Pie

Preheat oven to 350°F (*180°C*).

1 unbaked 9″ (*22 cm*) pie shell

¼ cup (*50 mL*) brown sugar
¼ cup (*50 mL*) white sugar
1½ cups (*375 mL*) corn syrup
— Combine in saucepan, stir and bring to boil.

Remove from heat.

¼ cup (*50 mL*) butter — Add butter and mix well.

Let sit until slightly cooled.

3 eggs — Beat eggs together, then add to mixture, beating well.

1 cup (*250 mL*) salted peanuts, chopped
1 tsp. (*5 mL*) vanilla
— Add and pour into unbaked shell.

Bake for 45 minutes.

A recession pecan pie.

Peanut Butter Nanaimo Bars

Layer One

½ cup (*125 mL*) butter
¼ cup (*50 mL*) sugar
1 egg
1 tsp. (*5 mL*) vanilla
1 Tbsp. (*15 mL*) cocoa

} Mix together and set over boiling water until *slightly* thickened. Stir occasionally.

2 cups (*500 mL*) graham cracker crumbs
1 cup (*250 mL*) dessicated coconut
½ cup (*125 mL*) peanuts, chopped

} Mix and add to above.

Press into buttered 9″ (*22 cm*) square pan so that base is evenly spread. Chill 15 minutes.

Layer Two

½ cup (*125 mL*) peanut butter
2 Tbsp. (*30 mL*) soft butter
2 Tbsp. (*30 mL*) custard powder
2 cups (*500 mL*) icing sugar
4 Tbsp. (*60 mL*) milk

} Mix well together and spread over Layer One.

Chill for 15 minutes.

Layer Three

4–5 oz. (*115–140 g*) semi-sweet chocolate
1 Tbsp. (*15 mL*) butter

} Melt over hot water and spread over Layer Two.

Chill. Score chocolate with sharp paring knife, then cut into squares.

No sooner had The Lazy Gourmet invented this recipe than several bakeries tried to duplicate it. Here's the real thing.

Peanut Brittle

Butter large marble slab or two cookie sheets.

2 cups (*500 mL*) white sugar
1 cup (*250 mL*) brown sugar
1¾ cups (*425 mL*) light corn syrup
1 cup (*250 mL*) water

In heavy saucepan, combine and cook until candy thermometer reads 240°F (*115°C*).

5 cups (*1.25 L*) raw peanuts

Add and cook until thermometer reaches 295°F (*145°C*).

2 Tbsp. (*30 mL*) butter

Remove from heat and add.

2 tsp. (*10 mL*) baking soda
½ tsp. (*2 mL*) salt

Add and beat mixture vigorously.

Pour onto slab or sheets, spreading as thinly as possible. When cool, break up. Makes about 4 dozen pieces.

If you are feeling experimental, try making this with other nuts or spreading the brittle with melted chocolate.

Peanut Butter Crispy Squares

½ cup (*125 mL*) sugar
½ cup (*125 mL*) corn syrup } Combine and heat until mixture boils. Remove from heat.

½ cup (*125 mL*) peanut butter
½ tsp. (*2 mL*) vanilla } Add and mix well.

3 cups (*750 mL*) rice crisp cereal
1 cup (*250 mL*) peanuts, coarsely chopped } Stir into above mixture until everything is coated.

½ cup (*125 mL*) chocolate chips — Add chips last.

Pat into prepared 8″ (*20 cm*) square pan. Cool and cut into bars.

Great as a lunchbox snack or when you need to produce treats in a hurry.

Peanut Butter Truffles

1 cup (*250 mL*) crunchy peanut butter
4 Tbsp. (*60 mL*) soft butter
1¼ cups (*300 mL*) icing sugar } Mix well and then form into balls.

Chill well or freeze.

6 oz. (*170 g*) semi-sweet chocolate, melted — Dip peanut butter balls in melted chocolate and set on waxed paper.

Chill before serving.

Peanut Butter Pinwheels

1¼ cups (*300 mL*) flour
¼ tsp (*1 mL*) salt
¼ tsp (*1 mL*) baking soda

Sift together.

½ cup (*125 mL*) soft butter — Cream well.
1 cup (*250 mL*) sugar — Add sugar.
½ cup (*125 mL*) peanut butter
1 egg
2 Tbsp. (*30 mL*) milk

Add peanut butter, egg and milk separately, mixing after each addition.

Now add flour mixture, mixing well.

Let chill 20 minutes. Divide into three pieces. Roll out ½" (*1 cm*) thick — not too thin or pinwheels will crumble.

3 oz. (*85 g*) semi-sweet chocolate, melted and slightly cooled

Spread dough with chocolate and roll up like a jelly roll.

Chill 30 minutes. Preheat oven to 350°F (*180°C*).

Slice into ¼" (*0.5 cm*) rounds and bake on buttered cookie sheet for 12–15 minutes, until golden. Makes about 4 dozen.

A pretty, crispy cookie.

Peanut Butter Chocolate Chip Cookies

Preheat oven to 350°F (*180°C*).

1 cup (*250 mL*) smooth peanut butter 1 cup (*250 mL*) soft butter	Beat well until soft and creamy.
⅔ cup (*150 mL*) white sugar ½ cup (*125 mL*) brown sugar	Add gradually and beat until fluffy.
2 eggs	Add eggs, one at a time, beating after each addition.
2½ cups (*625 mL*) flour 1 tsp. (*5 mL*) baking powder	Sift over mixture and stir until well blended.
1 cup (*250 mL*) chocolate chips	Add.
	Roll dough into balls. Press with back of fork onto lightly buttered cookie sheet.

Bake for 10 minutes until very light golden. Be careful not to over-bake. Makes 4 dozen.

What could be better than a combination of two favourites? These cookies freeze well — if they make it from the oven to the freezer.

PHOTO CREDITS

The publisher would like to thank the following people and companies for their assistance: Classy Formal Wear, Eaton's, Georg Jensen, Good Enough, Murdine Hirsch, Industrial Revolution, Inform, Kaya Kaya, Room Service, Tile Town, W. H. Puddifoot and World Mosaic.

Cover photograph: tuxedos courtesy of Classy Formal Wear, tiles from World Mosaic; page 17: cake dish courtesy of Kaya Kaya, silver (Cypress Sterling) from Georg Jensen; page 18: tiles courtesy of World Mosaic, lacquer tray from Room Service; page 35: cake platter courtesy of W. H. Puddifoot, shell plate from Room Service; page 36: silver courtesy of Georg Jensen, serving dish from Kaya Kaya; page 53: lacquer tray courtesy of Kaya Kaya, serviettes from Inform, and silver from Georg Jensen; page 54: champagne glasses courtesy of Inform, serviettes from Good Enough; page 71: silver courtesy of Georg Jensen; page 72: trays courtesy of Kaya Kaya, silver from Georg Jensen; page 89: lacquer bowls courtesy of Kaya Kaya; page 90: tray courtesy of Inform, serviettes from Good Enough.